easy **UKULELE TAB EDITION**

UKE 'AN PLAY
RADIOHEAD

Alfred

Produced by
Alfred Music Publishing Co., Inc.
P.O. Box 10003
Van Nuys, CA 91410-0003
alfred.com

ISBN-10: 0-7390-7861-5
ISBN-13: 978-0-7390-7861-7

 Alfred Cares. Contents printed on 100% recycled paper.

CONTENTS

15 STEP

Words and Music by
THOMAS YORKE, JONATHAN GREENWOOD,
COLIN GREENWOOD, EDWARD O'BRIEN and PHILIP SELWAY

15 Step - 5 - 1

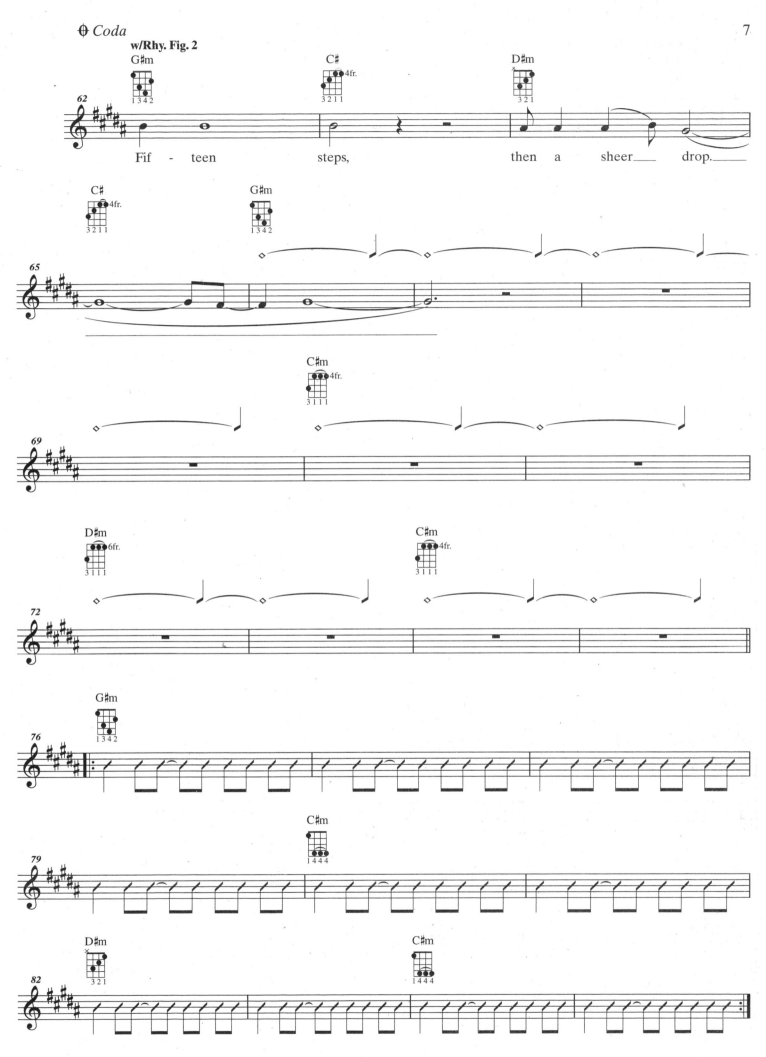

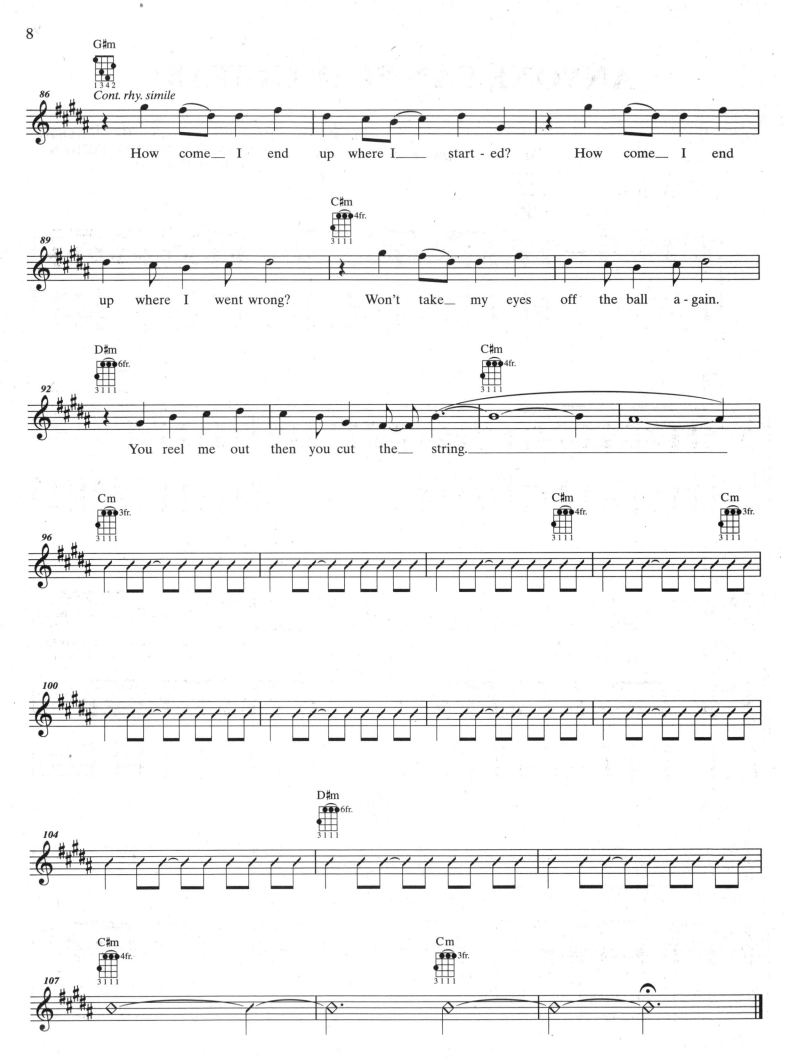

ANYONE CAN PLAY GUITAR

Words and Music by
THOMAS YORKE, JONATHAN GREENWOOD,
COLIN GREENWOOD, EDWARD O'BRIEN
and PHILIP SELWAY

Anyone Can Play Guitar - 3 - 1

BODYSNATCHERS

Words and Music by
THOMAS YORKE, JONATHAN GREENWOOD,
COLIN GREENWOOD, EDWARD O'BRIEN
and PHILIP SELWAY

Moderately fast ♩ = 168

Bodysnatchers - 6 - 1

1st time only

two   for   no.____

end Rhy. Fig. 1

w/Rhy. Fig. 1

I've   no____   i - dea____   what____   { I____   am }   talk -
                                              { you____   are }

- ing   a - bout.____

{ I'm   trapped____   in   this   bod - y   and   can't____   get
{ Your   mouth   moves____   on - ly   with____   some - one's   hand____   up   your

out. }
ass. }

Oh   oh   oh,__

Cont. in slashes

BLACK STAR

Words and Music by
THOMAS YORKE,
JONATHAN GREENWOOD, COLIN GREENWOOD,
EDWARD O'BRIEN and PHILIP SELWAY

Black Star - 3 - 1

CREEP

Words and Music by
THOMAS YORKE, JONATHAN GREENWOOD,
COLIN GREENWOOD, EDWARD O'BRIEN,
PHILIP SELWAY, ALBERT HAMMOND
and MIKE HAZELWOOD

Moderately ♩ = 92

Creep - 5 - 1

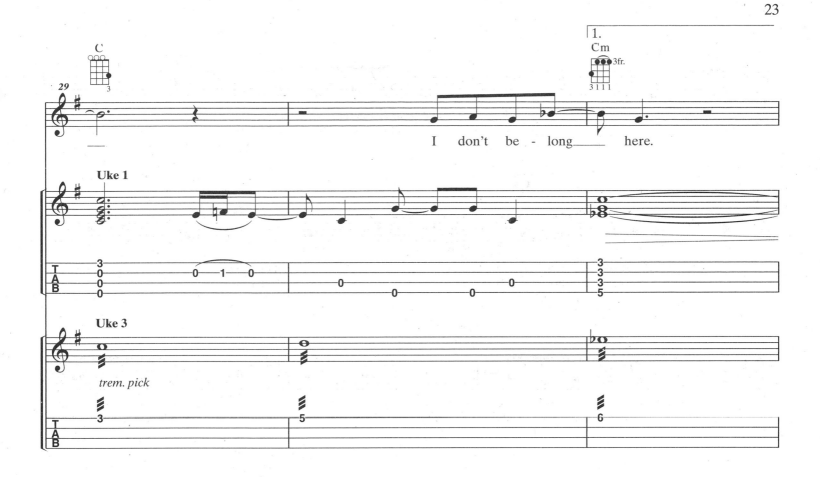

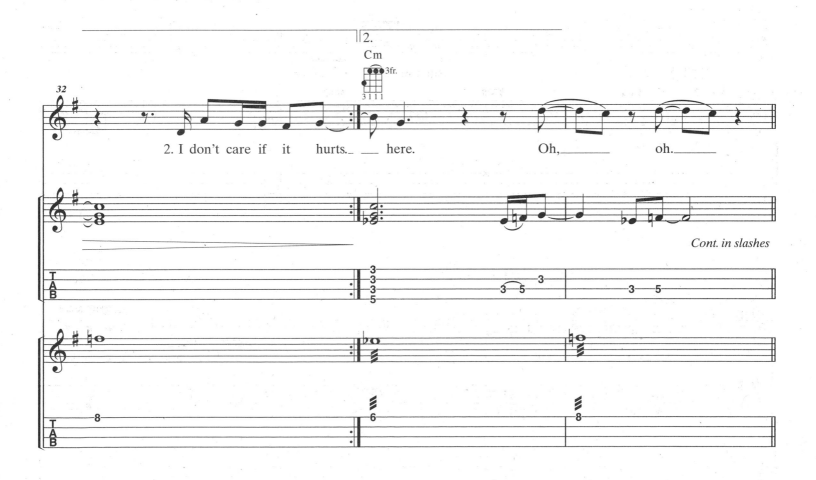

FAKE PLASTIC TREES

Moderately slow ♩ = 76

Verse:

Words and Music by
THOMAS YORKE, JONATHAN GREENWOOD,
COLIN GREENWOOD, EDWARD O'BRIEN
and PHILIP SELWAY

JUST

Words and Music by
THOMAS YORKE, JONATHAN GREENWOOD,
COLIN GREENWOOD, EDWARD O'BRIEN
and PHILIP SELWAY

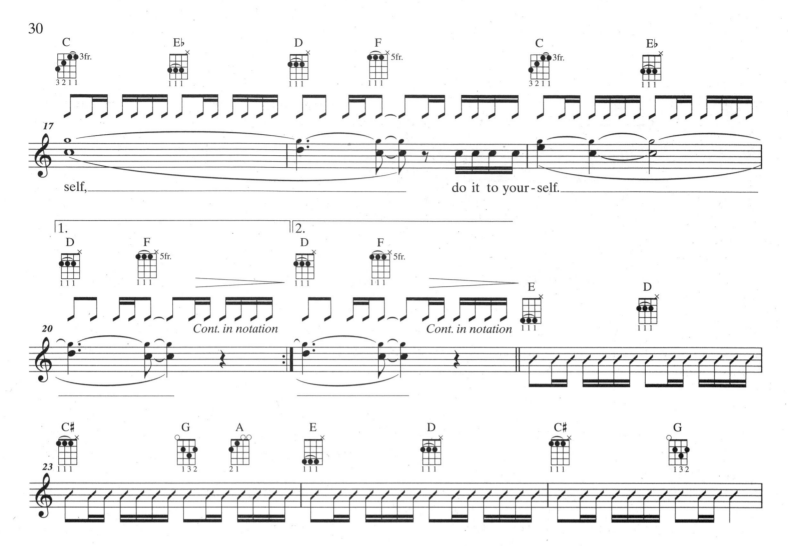

self,_____ do it to your-self._____

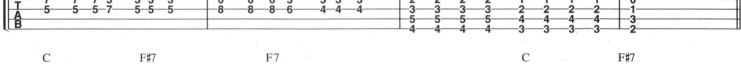

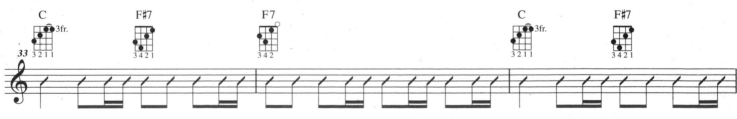

HIGH AND DRY

Words and Music by
THOMAS YORKE, JONATHAN GREENWOOD,
COLIN GREENWOOD, EDWARD O'BRIEN
and PHILIP SELWAY

Moderately slow ♩ = 86

Intro:

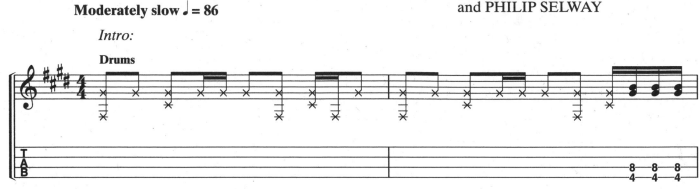

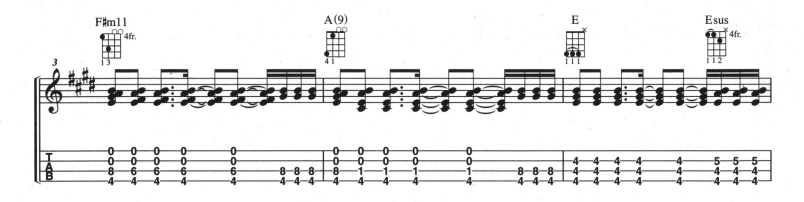

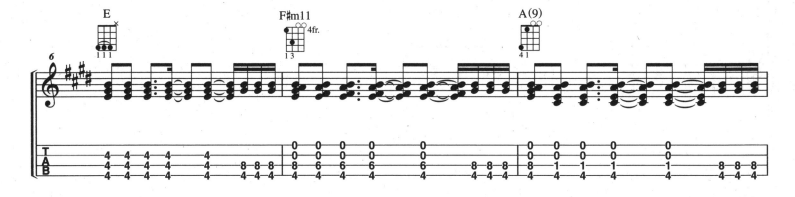

Cont. in slashes

High and Dry - 5 - 1

34

High and Dry - 5 - 3

Chorus:

Resume chorus rhy. simile

best thing you have had___ has gone_____ a - way.

So don't leave me high,_____ don't leave me dry.___

Don't leave me high,____

don't leave me dry._____ Don't leave me high,__

don't leave me high,__

don't leave me___ dry.___

KARMA POLICE

Words and Music by
THOMAS YORKE, JONATHAN GREENWOOD,
COLIN GREENWOOD, EDWARD O'BRIEN
and PHILIP SELWAY

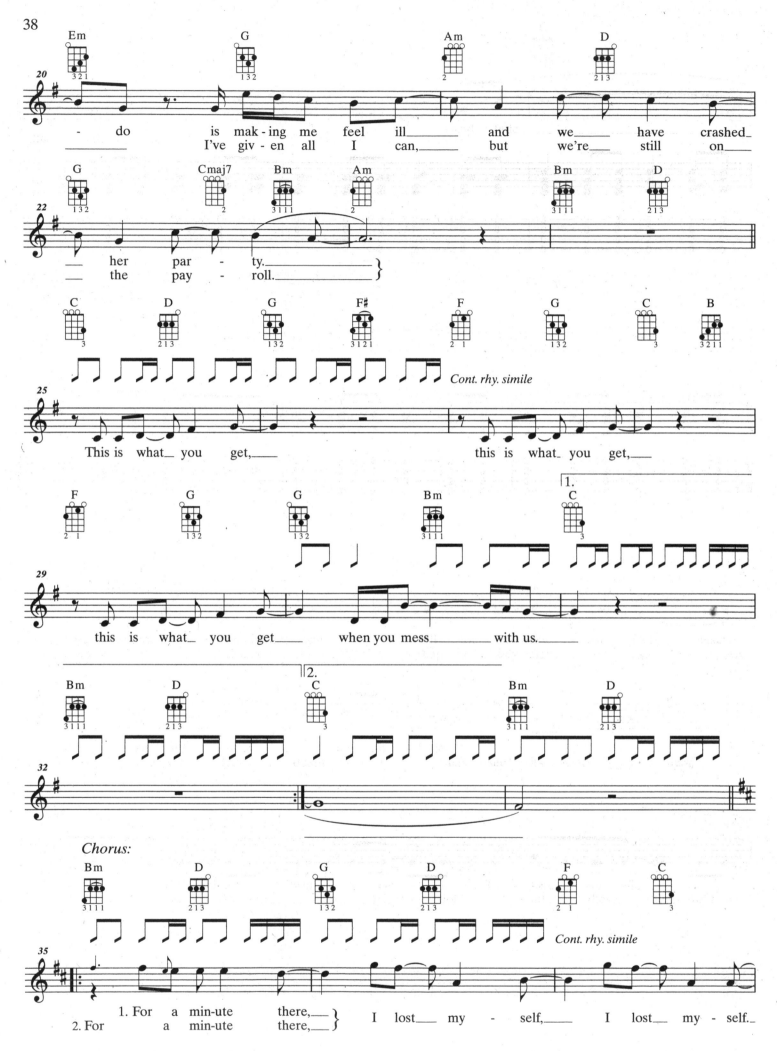

Phew, for a min - ute there,___ I lost___ my - self,___ I lost___ my - self.___

___ I lost___ my - self.___

KNIVES OUT

Words and Music by
THOMAS YORKE, JONATHAN GREENWOOD,
COLIN GREENWOOD, EDWARD O'BRIEN
and PHILIP SELWAY

Knives Out - 2 - 1

Look in - to my eyes._____ I'm
Look in - to my eyes,_____ it's the
bloat - ed and fro - zen. Still there's

not com - ing back._____
on - ly way you'll know I'm tell - ing_____ the truth._____
no point in let - ting it go to waste.

Chorus:

Cont. rhy. simile

So knives out,_____

1. catch the mouse._____
2. cook him up._____
3. catch the mouse._____

Don't look down___
Squash his head,___
Squash his head,___

To Coda

shove it in_____ your mouth.___
put him in_____ the pot.___
put him in_____ the pot.___

1.

2. *D.C. al Coda*

2. If

Coda
Em6

MY IRON LUNG

Words and Music by
THOMAS YORKE, JONATHAN GREENWOOD,
COLIN GREENWOOD, EDWARD O'BRIEN
and PHILIP SELWAY

My Iron Lung - 4 - 1

Cont. in slashes

𝄋 *Verses 2 & 3:*

Cont. rhy. simile

2. We're too young to fall a-sleep, too
3. Suck, suck your teen-age thumb,

cy-ni-cal to speak. We are los-ing it,
toi-let trained and dumb. When the pow-er runs out,

can't you tell? We scratch our e-ter-nal itch,
we'll just hum. This, this is our new song,

our twen-ti-eth cen-t'ry bitch, and we are grate-
just like the last one, a to-tal

NO SURPRISES

Words and Music by
THOMAS YORKE, JONATHAN GREENWOOD,
COLIN GREENWOOD, EDWARD O'BRIEN
and PHILIP SELWAY

Moderately slow ♩ = 75

No Surprises - 3 - 1

Chorus:

Such a pret-ty house,____ such____ a pret-ty gar-den. No____

____ a - larms____ and no_____ sur-pris - es. No a - larms____ and no_____ sur-pris - es.

No a - larms____ and no_____ sur-pris - es, please.____

rit.

NUDE

Words and Music by
**THOMAS YORKE, JONATHAN GREENWOOD,
COLIN GREENWOOD, EDWARD O'BRIEN**
and **PHILIP SELWAY**

STREET SPIRIT (FADE OUT)

Words and Music by
THOMAS YORKE, JONATHAN GREENWOOD,
COLIN GREENWOOD, EDWARD O'BRIEN
and PHILIP SELWAY

Moderately fast ♩ = 136

Street Spirit (Fade Out) - 4 - 1

THERE THERE

Words and Music by
THOMAS YORKE, JONATHAN GREENWOOD,
COLIN GREENWOOD, EDWARD O'BRIEN
and PHILIP SELWAY

1. In pitch dark I go walk - ing in your land - scape.
2. There's al - ways a si - ren sing - ing you to

ship-wreck.____
*(Don't reach out, don't reach out. Don't reach out, don't reach out.)
*Background vocals on repeat only.

There There - 4 - 1

58

WEIRD FISHES/ARPEGGI

Words and Music by
THOMAS YORKE, JONATHAN GREENWOOD,
COLIN GREENWOOD, EDWARD O'BRIEN
and PHILIP SELWAY

Moderately fast ♩ = 152

Intro:
Drums

*Optional frame for strumming.

Weird Fishes/Arpeggi - 5 - 1

Verse 1:

In the deep - est o - cean,
Why should I____ stay_____ here?   the

bot - tom of the sea,
Why__ should I_____   stay?   your eyes,__

*I hit the bot - tom, hit the bot-

*Vocal on repeats only.

- tom and___ es - cape,___ es - cape.

Yeah,___

Yeah,